BABY BLUES® **14** SCRAPBOOK

MOTHERHOOD
IS NOT FOR WIMPS

Other Baby Blues® books from Andrews McMeel Publishing

Guess Who Didn't Take a Nap?
I Thought Labor Ended When the Baby Was Born
We Are Experiencing Parental Difficulties. . . Please Stand By
Night of the Living Dad
I Saw Elvis in My Ultrasound
One More and We're Outnumbered!
Check, Please. . .
threats, bribes & videotape
If I'm a Stay-At-Home Mom, Why Am I Always in the Car?
Lift and Separate
I Shouldn't Have to Scream More Than Once!

Treasuries

The Super-Absorbent Biodegradable Family-Size Baby Blues®
Baby Blues®: Ten Years and Still in Diapers

BABY BLUES® 14 SCRAPBOOK

MOTHERHOOD
IS NOT FOR WIMPS

BY RICK KIRKMAN
AND JERRY SCOTT

Andrews McMeel
Publishing

Kansas City

04 05 BAH 10 9 8 7 6 5

ISBN: 0-7407-1393-0

Library of Congress Catalog Card Number: 00-108457

Find *Baby Blues* on the Web at
www.babyblues.com

To Jeff, Michele, and Olivia. Sano y salvo.
—J.S.

To Sukey with true love and admiration.
In remembrance of Irving Phillips . . . thank you for showing me the way.
—R.K.

...DS ARE ...NG UP SO ...ST!

YEAH...

AT FIRST THEY'RE HELPLESS LITTLE THINGS DEMANDING YOUR ATTENTION, AND THEN THE NEXT THING YOU KNOW...

...THEY'RE HELPLESS **BIG** THINGS DEMANDING YOUR ATTENTION.

WHENEVER MY BIOLOGICAL CLOCK RINGS, I CAN ALWAYS COUNT ON MY SISTER TO HIT THE SNOOZE BUTTON FOR ME.

MOM! MOM! MOM! MOM! MOM! MOM!

WOULD YOU LIKE A COOKIE, HAMMIE?

IF HE GETS ONE, I GET ONE, TOO!!

MMM!

HOW ABOUT A STORY?

IF HE GETS ONE, I GET ONE, TOO!!

AND NOW I'M GOING TO GIVE YOU A NICE, WARM...

IF HE GETS ONE, I GET ONE, TOO!!

...BATH.

OHHHH.

WAAAAAAA! HAMMIE BIT ME!

HAMMIE, WE DO **NOT** BITE PEOPLE!

BITING IS A **NO-NO!**

EVEN A LITTLE BITE IS WRONG!

EVEN IF YOU'RE MAD IT'S WRONG!

THAT'S RIGHT!

THAT'S RIGHT!

THAT'S RIGHT!

EVEN IF SOMEBODY PUTS PEANUT BUTTER AND JELLY ON HER ARM AND **DARES** YOU, IT'S **WRONG!**

THAT'S RI—

WHAT??

NEVER MIND.

KIRKMAN & SCOTT

YAWN! I'M GOING TO BED.

OH, NO YOU'RE NOT, BUDDY.

GET DOWN HERE AND START ADDRESSING SOME OF THESE CHRISTMAS CARDS.

BUT IT'S ELEVEN-THIRTY!

SO?? IT'S ALSO DECEMBER THIRTEENTH, AND IF WE DON'T GET THESE OUT PRETTY SOON, OUR FRIENDS WILL TOTALLY FORGET WHO WE ARE!

SPEAKING OF THAT, WHO ARE **THESE** PEOPLE?

I DON'T KNOW, BUT THEY SEND US A CARD EVERY YEAR. JUST KEEP WRITING.

DID I HEAR DADDY COME IN?

YEAH... AND GUESS WHAT?

FWWWEEEEEET!

HE BOUGHT YOU WHISTLES?

AWWWW... WHO TOLD YOU?

MAY I BE EXCUSED?

NOT UNTIL YOU EAT MORE OF YOUR CASSEROLE.

I THINK I'LL GET SOME MORE CASSEROLE.

JUDGING BY YOUR WAISTLINE, I WONDER IF THAT'S A GOOD IDEA.

LUCKY DUCK.

LUCKY DUCK.

20

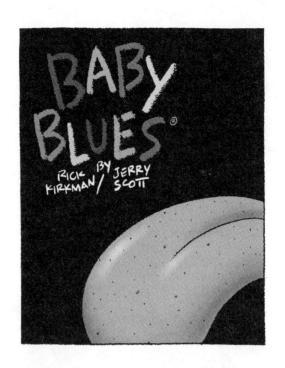

What goes around, comes around... usually a little too quickly.

FIVE MORE BITES OF THIS STUFF AND I GET DESSERT.

ULP! CHOKE! GAG! AAACK!

BLEAH!!

FOUR MORE BITES OF THIS STUFF AND I GET DESSERT...

AND YOUR DAD WONDERS WHY WE HAVE MACARONI THREE NIGHTS A WEEK.

KIRKMAN & SCOTT

HMMPH! MOM SAID THAT I'M BOSSY!

I'M **NOT** BOSSY! I HATE IT WHEN SHE SAYS I'M BOSSY! NOBODY ELSE THINKS I'M BOSSY! DO **YOU** THINK I'M BOSSY?

SAY, "NO."

NO.

SEE???

KIRKMAN & SCOTT

YOU KNOW MITCHELL FROM SCHOOL? I THINK HE LIKES ME.

OH? WHAT MAKES YOU THINK SO?

WELL, TODAY AT LUNCH, HE THREW A DIRT CLOD AT ME, BUT HE MISSED.

OH DEAR!

KIRKMAN & SCOTT

IS THAT THE WAY MITCHELL LETS SOMEBODY KNOW THAT HE LIKES THEM... BY THROWING DIRT CLODS AT THEM?

NO...

...IT ONLY MEANS HE LIKES YOU IF HE MISSES.

28

LOOK, HAMMIE! IF YOU DO THIS, YOU CAN CATCH SNOWFLAKES ON YOUR TONGUE!

BLECCH!

NOPE, THEY ONLY COME IN ONE FLAVOR.

WOO-HOOOO! IT'S THE WEEKEND! NO WORK!

NO SCHOOL!

YAY!

NOTHING TO DO BUT SIT AROUND AND RELAX!

AHHH!

AH!

MAN, AM I BORED.

ME, TOO

Z

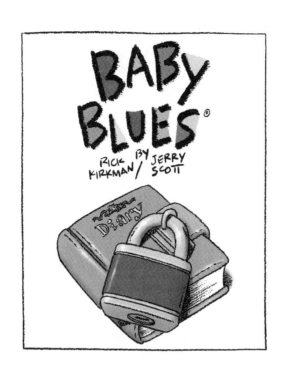

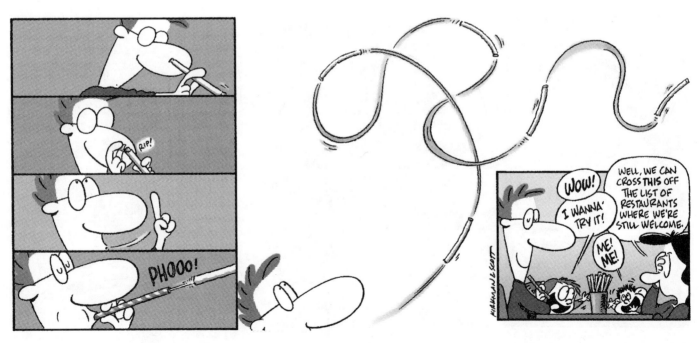

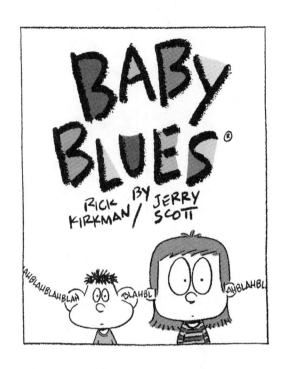

DON'T MOVE, DADDY! THERE'S A SPIDER ON YOU!

BAP! WAP! KONK! THWAP! BONK!

YOU HAVE TO BE CAREFUL... THOSE THINGS CAN HURT YOU!

MMMM! SLURP! SLURP! THIS SOUP IS GOOD! M!

I'M GLAD YOU LIKE IT. IT'S CREAM OF BROCCOLI.

THERE'S NOTHING WORSE THAN FINDING OUT THAT YOU LIKE SOMETHING YOU HATE!

PTHOOEY!

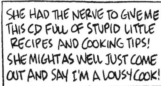

OOF! UNGH! UMMPH!

AAARG! OOH! OOH! BOOF!

YAY! HEE! HEE! HEE!

THANK YOU.

THANK YOU.

AND NOW, HERE'S WHAT IT SOUNDS LIKE WHEN **MOMMY** GETS OUT OF BED IN THE MORNING.

OTHER PEOPLE GET BALLET RECITALS AND ART SHOWS... **WE** GET A KID WHO DOES IMPRESSIONS.

KIRKMAN & SCOTT

HAMMIE, CAN YOU PICK UP YOUR TOY FOR DADDY?

PICK IT UP. COME ON, SON. YOU CAN DO IT. PICK IT UP. PICK IT UP. THAT'S IT. GO ON. PICK IT UP. PICK IT UP.

RIGHT HERE, SON. PICK UP THE TRUCK. PICK IT UP. YOU CAN DO IT. COME ON, PICK IT UP. PICKUPTHE TRUCKPICKUPTHETRUCKPICKUP THETRUCK.

KIRKMAN & SCOTT

WHAT'S GOING ON?

ARRRRRGH!

HAMMIE'S LEARNING TO IGNORE DADDY.

BAM! CRASH! OW!

YOU CAN'T CATCH ME! HEY! WHY, YOU... BANG!

HEY! WHAT'S GOING ON? WHY IS IT SO QUIET IN THERE?

CRASH! THONK!

LOOK OUT! BAM! HA! HA! HA! GIMME THAT! MINE!

I THINK THEY DO THAT JUST TO BUG ME.

RANDOM ACTS OF SILENCE.

KIRKMAN & SCOTT

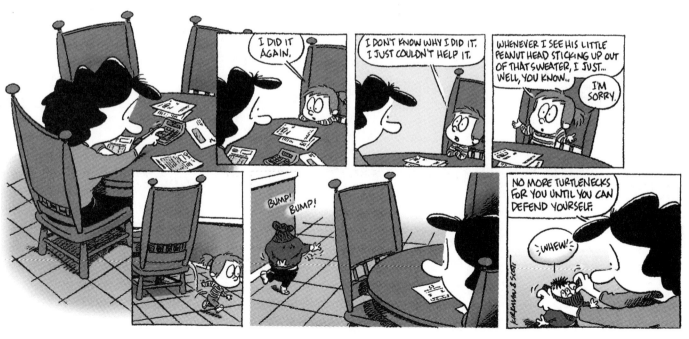

73

I DON'T KNOW WHAT TO PAINT.

PAINT A COWBOY.

AAAGH! THIS IS A TERRIBLE COWBOY!

IT'S BAD! IT'S STUPID! IT'S THE WORST PICTURE I EVER PAINTED AND IT'S ALL YOUR FAULT!

RIP!

SPLAT!

NOW WHAT SHOULD I PAINT?

ANYTHING BUT A COWBOY.

TODAY A KID NAMED MATTHEW SAID THAT HIS MOMMY IS PRETTIER THAN MY MOMMY.

AND WHAT DID YOU SAY?

I SAID SHE IS NOT, AND HE SAID SHE IS, TOO.

AND I SAID, IS NOT, AND HE SAID, IS, TOO, AND I SAID, IS NOT, AND HE SAID, IS, TOO, AND I SAID, IS NOT, AND PUNCHED HIM IN THE STOMACH.

I LIKE TO KEEP MY ARGUMENTS SHORT.

I DON'T HAVE A DOG! WHAT AM I SUPPOSED TO DO WITH A DOG HOUSE?

87

OH! THAT'S SO CUTE! I SHOULD MAKE A NOTE IN HAMMIE'S BABY BOOK!

I MEAN, I WOULD IF I COULD REMEMBER WHERE I PUT IT. AND IF I COULD FIND A PEN. AND IF THAT PEN HAD ANY INK IN IT. AND IF I HAD THIRTY UNINTERRUPTED SECONDS TO PUT TOGETHER A COHERENT SENTENCE...

SIGH! THE PAGES OF A SECOND CHILD'S BABY BOOK ARE FILLED WITH GOOD INTENTIONS.

ZOE! HAMMIE! WASH YOUR HANDS BEFORE DINNER!

AND USE SOAP THIS TIME!

NOW SIT UP STRAIGHT AND EAT YOUR VEGETABLES!

DON'T TALK WITH YOUR MOUTH FULL!

USE YOUR NAPKIN!

THERE YOU GO, MOM. NOW YOU CAN TAKE THE REST OF THE NIGHT OFF.

VERY FUNNY.

SNICKER!

I SEE LONDON! I SEE FRANCE! I SEE HAMMIE'S UNDERPANTS!

HA! HA! HA! HA! HA! HA! HA! HA! HA! HA!

OKAY.

THAT SONG IS A LOT FUNNIER IF THE PERSON YOU'RE SINGING ABOUT ISN'T WALKING AROUND IN A DIAPER.

HAPPY FATHER'S DAY!

WOW! WHAT'S ALL THIS?

WELL, WE MADE YOU SOME COLD TOAST AND WEAK COFFEE.

OH, GOODIE.

AND AFTER YOU OPEN YOUR PRESENTS, WE'RE GOING TO DISAPPEAR FOR A WHILE, LEAVING YOU TO CLEAN UP THE INCREDIBLE MESS WE LEFT IN THE KITCHEN.

HUH?

THEN WE'RE GOING TO PIN A HUGE UGLY FLOWER ON YOUR SHIRT AND TAKE YOU OUT TO BRUNCH AT A BIG, IMPERSONAL HOTEL RESTAURANT WHERE THEY SERVE VATS OF RUNNY SCRAMBLED EGGS AND UNDERCOOKED BACON THAT TASTE LIKE THEY WERE PREPARED IN A PRISON KITCHEN, AND, OF COURSE, THEY'LL HAVE CHAMPAGNE BY THE PITCHER.

THIS IS BEGINNING TO SOUND A LOT LIKE WHAT WE DID FOR MOTHER'S DAY...

♪TURNABOUT IS FAIR PLAY!♪

GET DRESSED! LET'S GO!

YAY!

DON'T FORGET THAT ZOE'S KINDERGARTEN GRADUATION IS TOMORROW.

GRADUATION "CEREMONY"? FOR KINDERGARTNERS??

OF COURSE! IT'S A REALLY BIG DEAL, TOO. CAPS AND GOWNS... POMP AND CIRCUMSTANCE... DIPLOMAS... THE WHOLE THING!

FOR KINDERGARTNERS??

RUMOR HAS IT THAT THE COMMENCEMENT SPEAKER IS BARNEY, THE DINOSAUR!

ISN'T THIS EXCITING!

YEAH, IT'S PRETTY CUTE.

CUTE?? IT'S A MILESTONE IN YOUR DAUGHTER'S LIFE!

THIS CEREMONY MARKS THE BEGINNING OF OUR DAUGHTER'S TRANSITION FROM A LITTLE GIRL TO AN EDUCATED, WORLDLY YOUNG WOMAN!

NOW WHERE IS SHE? I WANT TO GET ANOTHER PICTURE.

THIRD FROM THE LEFT... THE EDUCATED, WORLDLY YOUNG WOMAN PULLING THE WEDGIE OUT OF HER PANTIES.

...AND, ON THIS MOMENTOUS OCCASION, I'M REMINDED OF A FABLE INVOLVING A SMALL BOY AND HIS PET CHICKEN, WHO...

...THAT WE WOULD DO WELL TO REMEMBER THE WORDS OF THE POET WHO SO ELOQUENTLY...

SLAP!

...AS A MEMBER OF THE SCHOOL BOARD, I HAVE HAD THE OPPORTUNITY TO MEET ACTUAL STUDENTS ON OCCASION, AND...

ISN'T THIS THE MOST EXCITING GRADUATION CEREMONY YOU'VE EVER SEEN?

...PASTE, CRAYONS AND SCISSORS REPRESENT MUCH MORE THAN...

IT'S HAD ITS MOMENTS.

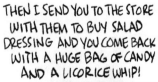

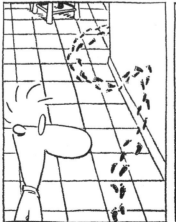

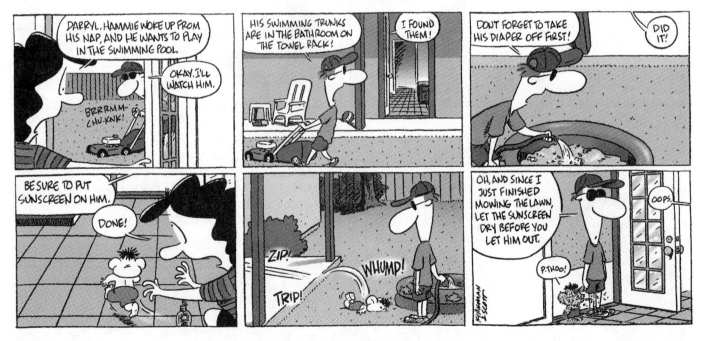

Don't look now, but you've **GOT** to see that family over there!

WHERE?

I just got a glimpse of them, but talk about your small-town goobers!

SHHHH! They'll hear you!

The guy is probably about my age, but he looks like he hasn't exercised in about five years...

YEAH?

And the wife isn't much better! She has bags under her eyes that wouldn't qualify as carry-on luggage, and a hairstyle that went out in the eighties!

REALLY?

Oh! And to complete the ensemble, they're dragging a couple of messy, snot-nosed kids along in a wagon!

A WAGON??

I think I'm going to cry.